The GEOLOGIC STORY of
the GREAT PLAINS

By DONALD E. TRIMBLE

A nontechnical description of the origin and evolution of the landscape of the Great Plains

Reprint with minor revisions of
GEOLOGICAL SURVEY BULLETIN 1493

Theodore Roosevelt
Nature and History Association
P.O. Box 167
Medora, ND 58645

Reprinted, with minor revisions, by Theodore Roosevelt Nature and
History Association, 1990, with permission from the United States
Department of the Interior, United States Geological Survey Office.
Originally printed in 1980 as Geological Survey Bulletin 1493.
Sixth printing in 2013.

Cover design by Barnstorm Design Creative,
        Colorado Springs, Colorado 80904.

Printed in the USA by The Printers, Inc.,
        Bismarck, North Dakota 58504.

ISBN 0-9601652-8-2

Library of Congress Cataloging in Publication Data
Trimble, Donald E.
The geologic story of the Great Plains.
(U.S. Geological Survey Bulletin 1493)
Bibliography: p. 50
Includes index.
Supt. of Docs. no.: I 19.3: 1493
1. Geology – Great Plains. I. Title.
II. Series: United States Geological Survey Bulletin 1493.
QE75.B9 no. 1493 [QE71] 557.3s [557.8] 80-607022

Theodore Roosevelt Nature and History Association was organized
in 1951 to aid and promote the historical, scientific, and
educational activities of the National Park Service. As a non-
profit organization authorized by Congress, it makes interpretive
material available to park visitors by sale or free distribution. All
net proceeds support the interpretive and research programs of
the National Park Service in North Dakota.

Contents

Figures

Figures

Table

The GEOLOGIC STORY of the GREAT PLAINS

By DONALD E. TRIMBLE

Introduction

The Great Plains! The words alone create a sense of space and a feeling of destiny – a challenge. But what exactly is this special part of Western America that contains so much of our history? How did it come to be? Why is it different?

Geographically, the Great Plains is an immense sweep of country; it reaches from Mexico far north into Canada and spreads out east of the Rocky Mountains like a huge welcome mat. So often maligned as a drab, featureless area, the Great Plains is in fact a land of marked contrasts and limitless variety: canyons carved into solid rock of an arid land by the waters of the Pecos and the Rio Grande; the seemingly endless grainfields of Kansas; the desolation of the Badlands; the beauty of the Black Hills.

Before it was broken by the plow, most of the Great Plains from the Texas panhandle northward was treeless grassland. Trees grew only along the floodplains of streams and on the few mountain masses of the northern Great Plains. These lush prairies once were the grazing ground for immense herds of bison, and the land provided a bountiful life for those Indians who followed the herds. South of the grasslands, in Texas, shrubs mixed with the grasses: creosote bush along the valley of the Pecos River; mesquite, oak, and juniper to the east.

1

The general lack of trees suggests that this is a land of little moisture, as indeed it is. Nearly all of the Great Plains receives less than 24 inches of rainfall a year, and most of it receives less than 16 inches. This dryness and the strength of sunshine in this area, which lies mostly between 2,000 and 6,000 feet above sea level, create the semiarid environment that typifies the Great Plains. But it was not always so. When the last continental glacier stood near its maximum extent, some 12,000-14,000 years ago, spruce forest reached southward as far as Kansas, and the Great Plains farther south was covered by deciduous forest. The trees retreated northward as the ice front receded, and the Great Plains has been a treeless grassland for the last 8,000-10,000 years.

For more than half a century after Lewis and Clark crossed the country in 1805-6, the Great Plains was the testing ground of frontier America – here America grew to maturity (fig. 1). In 1805-7, explorer Zebulon Pike crossed the southcentral Great Plains, following the Arkansas River from near Great Bend, Kans., to the Rocky Mountains. In later years, Santa Fe traders, lured by the wealth of New Mexican trade, followed Pike's path as far as Bents Fort, Colo., where they turned southwestward away from the river route. Those pioneers who later crossed the plains on the Oregon Trail reached the Platte River near the place that would become Kearney, Nebr., by a nearly direct route from Independence, Mo., and followed the Platte across the central part of the Great Plains.

Although these routes may have seemed long and tedious to those dusty travelers, they provided relatively easy access to the Rocky Mountains and had a continuous supply of fresh water, an absolute necessity in these plains. The minds of those frontiersmen surely were occupied with the dangers and demands of the moment – and with dreams – but the time afforded by the slow pace of travel also gave them ample opportunity for thought about the origins of their surroundings.

Today's traveler, who has less time for contemplation, races past a changing kaleidoscope of landscape. The increased awareness created by this rapidity of change perhaps is even more likely to stimulate questions about the origin of this landscape.

Figure 1. – Index map of the Great Plains showing route of Lewis and Clark and the Santa Fe and Oregon Trails.

For instance, the westbound traveler on Interstate Highway 70 traverses nearly a thousand miles of low, rounded hills after leaving the Appalachians; the rolling landscape is broken only by a few flat areas where glacial ice or small lakes once stood. Suddenly, near Salina, Kans., the observant traveler senses a difference in the landscape. Instead of rounded hills, widely or closely spaced, he sees on the skyline flat surfaces, or remnants of flat surfaces. As he climbs gently westward these broken horizontal lines stand etched against the sky. About 35 miles west of Salina he finds himself on a broad, flat plateau, where seemingly he can see forever. Truc, in places he descends into stream valleys, but only briefly, for he soon climbs back onto the flat surface.

This plateau surface continues for 300 miles to the west – to within 100 miles of the abrupt front of the Rocky Mountains. East-flowing streams, such as the Smoky Hill, the Saline, the Solomon, and the Republican Rivers and their tributary branches, have cut their valleys into this surface, but these valleys become increasingly shallow and disappear entirely near the western rim of the plateau in eastern Colorado.

The distant peaks of the Rockies are seen for the first time as the traveler approaches the escarpment that forms the western edge of this great plateau. After crossing the escarpment near Limon, Colo., he begins the long gentle descent to Denver, on the South Platte River near the foot of the mountains that loom so awesomely ahead. He has crossed the Great Plains. The distances have been great, but the contrasts have been marked.

Had our traveler selected a different route, either to the north or south, he would have found even greater contrasts, for the Great Plains has many parts, each with its own distinctive aspect. Why should such diverse landscapes be considered parts of the Great Plains? What are their unifying features? And what created this landscape? Has it always been this way? If not, when was it formed? How was it formed?

We will look here at some of the answers to those questions. The history of events that produced the landscape of the Great Plains is interpreted both from the materials that compose the landforms and from the landforms themselves. As we will see, all landforms are the result of geologic processes in action. These processes determine not only the size and shape of the landforms, but also the materials of which they are made. These geologic processes, which form and shape our Earth's surface, are simply the inevitable actions of the restless interior of the Earth and of the air, water, and carbon dioxide of the atmosphere, aided by gravity and solar heating (or lack of it). They all have helped sculpture the fascinating diversity of the part of our land we call the Great Plains.

What is the Great Plains?

The United States has been subdivided into physiographic regions that, although they have great diversity within themselves, are distinctly different from each other (fig. 2).

From the Rocky Mountains on the west to the Appalachians on the east, the interior of our country is a vast lowland known as the Interior Plains. These plains are bounded on the south by a region of Interior Highlands, consisting of the Ozark Plateaus and the Ouachita province, and by the Coastal Plain. In the Great Lakes region, the Interior Plains laps onto the most ancient part of the continent, the Superior Upland. West of the Great Lakes it extends far to the north into Canada. Certainly the Rocky Mountains are distinctly different from the region to the east, which is the Great Plains. The Great Plains, then, is the western part of the great Interior Plains. The Rocky Mountains form its western margin. But what determines its eastern margin?

During the Pleistocene Epoch or Great Ice Age, huge glaciers formed in Canada and advanced southward into the great, central, low-lying Interior Plains of the United States. (See figure 2.) These glaciers and their deposits modified the surface of the land they covered, mostly between the Missouri and the Ohio Rivers; they smoothed the contours and gave the land a more subdued aspect that it had before they came. This glacially smoothed and modified land is called the Central Lowland. Although the ice sheets lapped onto the northern part, the Great Plains is the largely unglaciated region that extends from the Gulf Coastal Plain

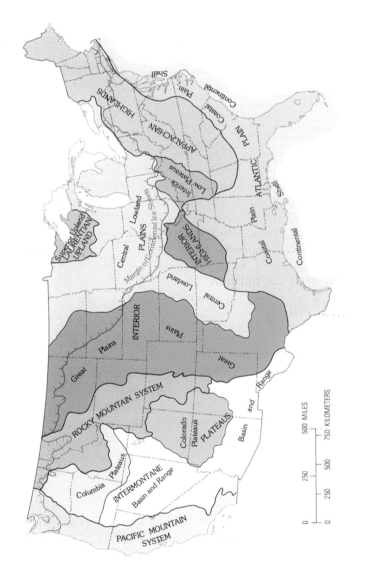

Figure 2. – Physical divisions of the United States and maximum extent of the continental ice sheets during the Great Ice Age.

in Texas northward into Canada between the Central Lowland and the foot of the Rocky Mountains. Its eastern margin in Texas and Oklahoma is marked by a prominent escarpment, the Caprock escarpment. Its southern margin, where it abuts the Coastal Plain in Texas, is at another abrupt rise or scarp along the Balcones fault zone.

The Great Plains – its parts

Within the Great Plains are many large areas that differ greatly from adjoining areas (fig. 3). The Black Hills stands out distinctively from the surrounding lower land, and its dark, forested prominence can be seen for scores of miles from any direction. At the southern end of the Great Plains is another, less imposing, forested prominence – the Central Texas Uplift. Most impressive, perhaps, is the huge, nearly flat plateau known as the High Plains, which extends southward from the northern border of Nebraska through the Panhandle of Texas, and which forms the central part of the Great Plains. The east and west rims of the southern High Plains are at high, cliffed, erosional escarpments – the Caprock escarpment on the east and the Mescalero escarpment on the west. The north edge of the High Plains is defined by another escarpment, the Pine Ridge escarpment, which separates the High Plains from a region that has been greatly dissected by the Missouri River and its tributaries. There, several levels of rolling upland are surmounted by small mountainous masses and flat-topped buttes and are entrenched by streams. This region is the Missouri Plateau. The continental glacier lapped onto the northeastern part of the Missouri Plateau and altered its surface.

The South Platte and Arkansas Rivers and their tributaries have similarly dissected an area along the mountain front that is called the Colorado Piedmont, and the Pecos River has excavated a broad valley trending southward from the Sangre de Cristo Mountains in New Mexico into Texas. The Mescalero escarpment separates the Pecos Valley from the southern High Plains (fig. 4). South and east of the Pecos

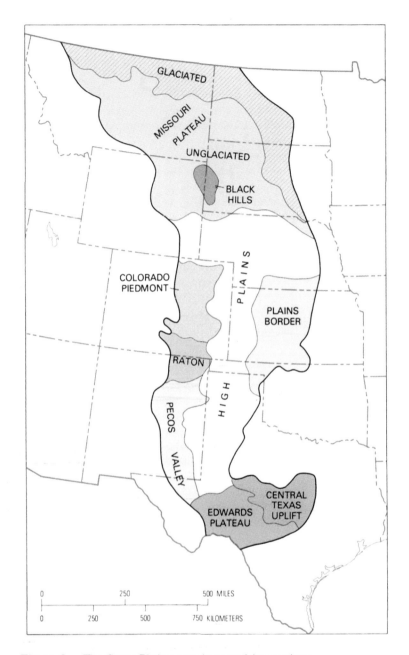

Figure 3. – The Great Plains province and its sections.

Figure 4. – Mescalero escarpment and the southern High Plains (Llano Estacado) south of Tucumcari, N. Mex. Photograph by C. D. Miller, U.S. Geological Survey.

Valley, extending to the Rio Grande and the Coastal Plain, is a broad plateau of bare, stripped, flat-lying limestone layers bearing little but cactus that is called the Edwards Plateau. Green, crop-filled valleys with gently sloping valley walls and rounded stream divides trend eastward from the High Plains of western Kansas and characterize a Plains Border section. And finally, between the Colorado Piedmont on the north and the Pecos Valley on the south, volcanic vents, cinder cones, and lava fields from another distinctive terrain in the part of the Great Plains called the Raton section.

Can such diverse parts of our land have a sufficiently common origin to justify their being considered part of one unified whole – the Great Plains? Probably so, but to understand why, we must examine some of the earlier geologic history of the Great Plains as well as subsequent events revealed in the present landforms. We will find that all parts of this region we call the Great Plains have a similar early history, and that the differences we see are the results of local dominance of certain processes in the ultimate shaping of the landscape, mostly during the last few million years. The distinctive character of the landscape in each section is determined in part by both the early events and the later shaping processes.

Early History

The Interior Plains, of which the Great Plains is the western, mostly unglaciated part (fig. 2), is the least complicated part of our continent geologically except for the Coastal Plain. For most of the half billion years from 570 million (fig. 5) until about 70 million years ago, shallow seas lay across the interior of our continent (fig. 6). A thick sequence of layered sediments, mostly between 5,000 and 10,000 feet thick, but more in places, was deposited onto the subsiding floor of the interior ocean (table 1). These sediments, now consolidated into rock, rest on a floor of very old rocks that are much like the ancient rocks of the Superior Upland.

About 70 million years ago the seas were displaced from the continental interior by slow uplift of the continent, and the landscape that appeared was simply the extensive, nearly flat floor of the former sea.

Warping and stream deposition

Most of these rocks of marine origin lie at considerable depth beneath the land surface, concealed by an overlying thick, layered sequence of rocks laid down by streams, wind, and glaciers. Nevertheless, their geologic character, position, and form are exceptionally well known from information gained from thousands of wells that have been drilled for oil. The initial, nearly horizontal position of the layers of rock beneath the Interior Plains has been little disturbed except where mountains like the Black Hills were uplifted about 70 million years ago. At those places, which are all in the northern and southern parts of the Great Plains, the sedimentary layers have been warped up and locally broken by the rise of hot molten rock from depth. Elsewhere in the Interior Plains, however, earth forces of about the same period caused only a reemphasis of gentle undulations in the Earth's crust.

These undulations affected both the older basement rocks and the overlying sedimentary rocks, and they take the form of gentle basins and arches that in some places span several States. (See sketch map, figure 7.) A series of narrow basins lies along the mountain front on the west side of the Great Plains. A broad, discontinuous arch extends southwest from the Superior Upland to the Rocky Mountain front to form a buried divide that separates the large Williston basin on the north from the Anadarko basin to the south.

While the flat-lying layers of the Interior Plains were being only gently warped, vastly different earth movements were taking place farther west, in the area of the present Rocky Mountains. Along a relatively narrow north-trending belt, extending from Mexico to Alaska, the land was being uplifted

Figure 5 (overleaf) – Geologic time chart and progression of life forms. Note Cretaceous Triceratops, Oligocene Titanotheres, and Miocene Moropus.

MESOZOIC

−200 M.Y. AGO

251 MILLION YEARS

TRIASSIC PERIOD   JURASSIC   PERIOD   CR

−542 M.Y. AGO   CAMBRIAN PERIOD   ORDOVICIAN   PERI

PALEOZOIC

PERMIAN PERIOD   PENNSYLVANIAN   PERIOD   MISSISSIPPIAN PERIOD   DE

PRECAMBRIAN ERA

11,500 YR.

GEOLOGIC TIME
The Age of the Earth

The Earth is very old – 4.5 billion years or more according to recent estimates. Most of the evidence for an ancient Earth is contained in the rocks that form the Earth's crust. The rock layers themselves – like pages in a long and complicated history – record the surface-shaping events of the past, and buried within them are traces of life – the plants and animals that evolved from organic structures that existed perhaps 3 billion years ago.

Also contained in rocks once molten are radioactive elements whose isotopes provide Earth scientists with an atomic clock. Within these rocks, "parent" isotopes decay at a predictable rate to form "daughter" isotopes. By determining the relative amounts of parent and daughter isotopes, the age of these rocks can be calculated.

Thus, the results of studies of rock layers (stratigraphy), and of fossils (paleontology), coupled with the ages of certain rocks as measured by atomic clocks (geochronology), attest to a very old Earth!

1 BILLION YEARS AGO

2 BILLION YEARS AGO

3 BILLION YEARS AGO
EARLIEST ORGANIC
STRUCTURES

4.5 BILLION
YEARS AGO

Triceratops

65 MILLION YEARS AGO

56 M.Y.

34 M.Y.

Paleocene Epoch

Eocene Epoch

EOUS PERIOD

TERTIARY PERIOD

SILURIAN PERIOD

IAN PERIOD

Moropus

Titanotheres

CENOZOIC ERA

Oligocene Epoch

Miocene Epoch

PERIOD

Oligocene Epoch

Pliocene Epoch

ocene poch

Pleistocene Epoch

TERTIARY

UATERNARY PERIOD

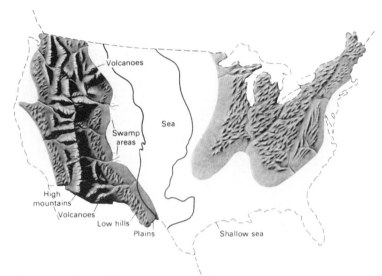

Figure 6. – *Generalized paleogeographic map of the United States in Late Cretaceous time (65 to 80 million years ago), when most of the Great Plains was beneath the sea.*

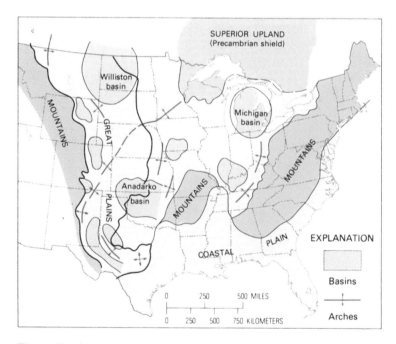

Figure 7. – *Structural setting of the Great Plains. Williston basin and Anadarko basin are separated by a midcontinental arch.*

Table 1. – Generalized chart of rocks of the Great Plains.

Geologic age		Millions of years Ago	Missouri Plateau-Black Hill	High Plains - Plains Border - Colorado Piedmont	Pecos Valley-Edwards Plateau - Central Texas
CENOZOIC	Quaternary — Pleistocene	2	Glacial deposits, alluvium, and terrace deposits	Alluvium, sand dunes, and loess	Pediment, terrace, and bolson deposits
	Quaternary — Pliocene	5			
	Tertiary — Miocene	22-24	Flaxville Gravel and Ogallala Formation	Ogallala Formation	
	Tertiary — Oligocene	37-38	Arikaree Formation	Arikaree Formation	Mostly missing because of erosion or nondeposition
	Tertiary — Eocene	53-54	White River Group / Wasatch and Golden Valley Formations	White River Group	
	Tertiary — Paleocene	65	Fort Union Formation	Denver, Poison Canyon, and Raton Formations	
MESOZOIC	Cretaceous	136	Hell Creek and Lance Formations / Fox Hills Sandstone / Shales, sandstones, and limestones deposited in Late Cretaceous sea. / Dakota Sandstone and Lakota Formation	Vermejo and Laramie Formations / Trinidad and Fox Hills Sandstones / Dakota Sandstone	Glen Rose and Edwards Limestones
	Jurassic	190-195	Sundance Formation, Ellis Group, and Unkpapa Sandstone	Morrison Formation	Jurassic rocks not present
	Triassic	225	Dominantly red rocks		
PALEOZOIC		570	Paleozoic rocks, undivided		
PRECAMBRIAN			Precambrian rocks, undivided		

15

at a great rate. The layers of sedimentary rock deposited in the inland sea were stripped from the crest of the rising mountainous belt by erosion and transported to its flanks as the gravel, sand, and mud of streams and rivers. This transported sediment was deposited on the plains to form the rocks of the Cretaceous Hell Creek, Lance, Laramie, Vermejo, and Raton Formations. Vegetation thrived on this alluvial plain, and thick accumulations of woody debris were buried to ultimately become coal. This lush vegetation provided ample food for the hordes of three-horned dinosaurs *(Triceratops)* that roamed these plains. Their fossilized remains are found from Canada to New Mexico.

As the mountains continued to rise, the eroding streams cut into the old core rocks of the mountains, and that debris too was carried to the flanks and onto the adjoining plains. The mountainous belt continued to rise intermittently, and volcanoes began to appear about 50 million years ago. Together, the mountains and volcanoes provided huge quantities of sediment, which the streams transported to the plains and deposited. The areas nearest the mountains were covered by sediments of Late Cretaceous and Paleocene age (table 1) – the Poison Canyon Formation to the south, the Dawson and Denver Formations in the Denver area, and the Fort Union Formation to the north (fig. 8). Vegetation continued to flourish, especially in the northern part of the Great Plains, and was buried to form the thick lignite and subbituminous coal beds of the Fort Union Formation (fig. 9). The earliest mammals, most of whose remains come from the Paleocene Fort Union Formation, have few modern survivors.

Beginning about 45 million years ago, in Eocene time, there was a long period of stability lasting perhaps 10 million years, when there was little uplift of the mountains and, therefore, little deposition on the plains. A widespread and strongly developed soil formed over much of the Great Plains during this period of stability. With renewed uplift and volcanism in the mountains at the end of this period, great quantities of sediment again were carried to the plains by streams and spread over the northern Great Plains and southeastward to the arch or divide separating the Williston and Anadarko basins (fig. 8). Those sediments form the White River Group, in which the South Dakota Badlands are

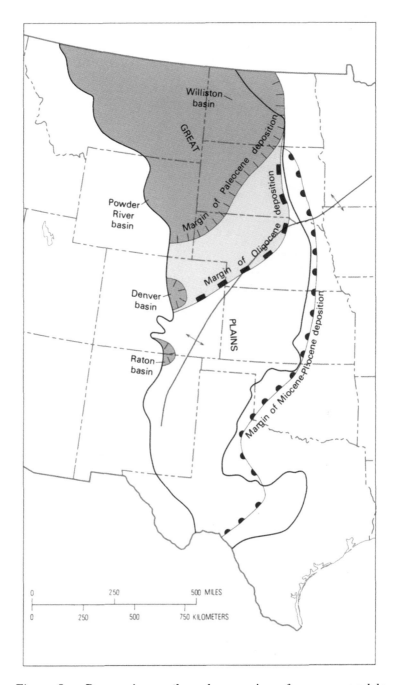

Figure 8. – Progressive southward expansion of areas covered by Paleocene, Oligocene, and Miocene-Pliocene sedimentary deposits.

Figure 9. – Big Horn coal strip mine in Fort Union Formation at Acme, Wyo. Photograph by F. W. Osterwald, U.S. Geological Survey.

carved. In addition to the *Titanotheres*, huge beasts with large, long horns on their snouts who lived only during the Oligocene (37 to 22 million years ago), vast herds of camels, rhinoceroses, horses, and tapirs – animals now found native only on other continents – grazed those Oligocene semiarid grassland plains.

Sometime between 20 and 30 million years ago the streams began depositing sand and gravel beyond the divide, and, for another 10 million years or more, stream sediments of the Arikaree and Ogallala Formations spread over the entire Great Plains from Canada to Texas, except where mountainous areas such as the Black Hills stood above the plains. Between 5 and 10 million years ago, then, the entire Great Plains was an eastward-sloping depositional plain surmounted only by a few mountain masses. Horses, camels, rhinoceroses, and a strange horselike creature with clawed feet (called *Moropus*) lived on this plain.

18

Sculpturing the land

Sometime between 5 and 10 million years ago, however, a great change took place, apparently as a result of regional uplift of the entire western part of the continent. While before, the streams had been depositing sediment on the plains for more than 60 million years, building up a huge thickness of sedimentary rock layers, now the streams were forced to cut down into and excavate the sediments they had formerly deposited. As uplift continued – and it may still be continuing – the streams cut deeper and deeper into the layered stack and developed tributary systems that excavated broad areas. High divides were left between streams in some places, and broad plateaus were formed and remain in other places. The great central area was essentially untouched by erosion and remained standing above the dissected areas surrounding it as the escarpment-rimmed plateau that is the High Plains.

This downcutting and excavation by streams, then, which began between 5 and 10 million years ago, roughed out the landscape of the Great Plains and created the sections we call the Missouri Plateau, the Colorado Piedmont, the Pecos Valley, the Edwards Plateau, and the Plains Border Section. Nearly all the individual landforms that now attract the eye have been created by geologic processes during the last 2 million years. It truly is a young landscape.

Landforms of today —

The surface features of the Great Plains

The mountainous sections of the Great Plains were formed long before the remaining areas were outlined by erosion. Uplift of the Black Hills and the Central Texas Uplift began as the continental interior was raised and the last Cretaceous sea was displaced, 65 to 70 million years ago. They stood well above the surrounding plains long before any sediments from the distant Rocky Mountains began to accumulate at their bases. In southern Colorado and northern New Mexico, molten rock invaded the sedimentary layers between 22 and

26 million years ago. The Spanish Peaks were formed at this time from hot magma that domed up the surface layers but did not break through; the magma has since cooled and solidified and has been exposed by erosion. Elsewhere the magma reached the surface, forming volcanoes, fissures, and basalt flows. A great thickness of basalt flows accumulated at Raton Mesa and Mesa de Maya between 8 and 2 million years ago. Volcanism has continued intermittently, and the huge cinder cone of Capulin Mountain was created by explosive eruption only 10,000 to 4,000 years ago. Most of these volcanic masses were formed before major downcutting by the streams began. Other igneous intrusions and volcanic areas in the northern Great Plains similarly were formed before the streams were incised.

To examine the origin of the present landscape and of the landforms typical of the various sections of the Great Plains, it is convenient to begin with the Black Hills, the Central Texas Uplift, and the Raton section simply because they were formed first – they existed before the other sections were outlined.

Black Hills

The Black Hills is a huge, elliptically domed area in northwestern South Dakota and northeastern Wyoming, about 125 miles long and 65 miles wide (fig. 10). Rapid City, S. Dak., is on the Missouri Plateau at the east edge of the Black Hills. Uplift caused erosion to remove the overlying cover of marine sedimentary rocks and expose the granite and metamorphic rocks that form the core of the dome. The peaks of the central part of the Black Hills presently are 3,000 to 4,000 feet above the surrounding plains. Harney Peak, with an altitude of 7,242 feet, is the highest point in South Dakota. These central spires and peaks all are carved from granite and other igneous and metamorphic rocks that form the core of the uplift. The heads of four of our great Presidents are sculpted from this granite at Mount Rushmore National Memorial. Joints in the rocks have controlled weathering processes that influenced the final shaping of many of these landforms. Closely spaced joints have produced the spires of the Needles area, and widely spaced joints have produced the rounded forms of granite that are seen near Sylvan Lake (fig. 11).

Marine sedimentary rocks surrounding the old core rocks form well-defined belts. Lying against the old core rocks and completely surrounding them are Paleozoic limestones that form the Limestone Plateau (fig. 10). These tilted layers have steep erosional scarps facing the central part of the Black Hills. Wind Cave and Jewel Cave were produced by ground water dissolving these limestones along joints. These caves

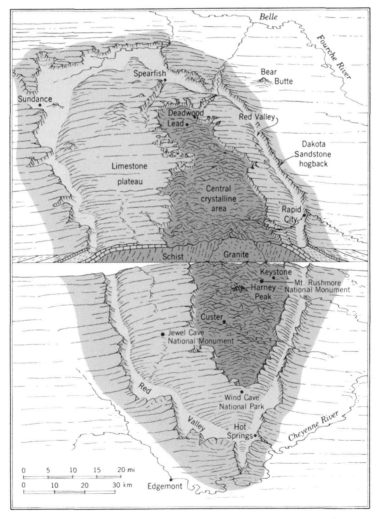

Figure 10. – Diagram of the Black Hills uplift by A. N. Strahler (Strahler and Strahler, 1978). Used by permission.

Figure 11. – Jointed granite rounded by weathering at Sylvan Lake, in the central part of the Black Hills, S. Dak. Photo courtesy of South Dakota Tourism.

are sufficiently impressive to be designated as a national park and a national monument, respectively. Encircling the Limestone Plateau is a continuous valley cut in soft Triassic shale. This valley has been called "the Racetrack," because of its continuity, and the Red Valley, because of its color. Surrounding the Red Valley is an outer hogback ridge formed by the tilted layers of the Dakota Sandstone, which are quite hard and resistant to erosion. Streams that flow from the central part of the Black Hills pass through the Dakota hogback in narrow gaps.

The Black Hills, then, is an uplifted area that has been carved deeply but differentially by streams to produce its major outlines. Those outlines have been modified mainly by weathering of the ancient core rocks and solution of the limestone of the Limestone Plateau.

Central Texas Uplift

The domed rocks of the Central Texas Uplift form a topography different from that of the Black Hills. Erosion of a broad, uplifted dome here has exposed a core of old granites, gneisses, and schists, as in the Black Hills, ι the Central Texas Uplift, erosion has produced a topograp basin, rather than high peaks and spires, on the old rock of the central area. A low plateau surface dissected into rounded ridges and narrow valleys slopes gently eastward from the edge of the central area to an escarpment at the Balcones fault zone, which determines the eastern edge of the Great Plains here. Northwest of the central basin the Colorado River flows in a broad lowland about 100 miles long, but the northern edge of the uplift, forming a divide between the Brazos and the Colorado Rivers, is a series of mesas formed of more resistant sandstone and limestone.

The cutting action of streams, modified or controlled in part by differences in hardness of the rock layers, has been responsible for the landforms of the Central Texas Uplift. Weathering of the old core rocks has softened them sufficiently to permit deeper erosion of the central area, and solution of limestone by ground water has formed such features as Longhorn Caverns, 11 miles southwest of Burnet, Tex.

Raton Section

Volcanism characterizes the Raton section. The volcanic rocks, which form peaks, mesas, and cones, have armored the older sedimentary rocks and protected them from the erosion that has cut deeply into the adjoining Colorado Piedmont to the north and Pecos Valley to the south. The south edge of the Raton section is marked by a spectacular south-facing escarpment cut on the nearly flat-lying Dakota Sandstone. This escarpment is the Canadian escarpment, north of the Canadian River. Northward for about 100 miles, the landscape is that of a nearly flat plateau cut on Cretaceous rock surmounted here and there by young volcanic vents, cones, and lava fields. Capulin Mountain is a cinder cone only 10,000 to 4,000 years old (fig. 12). Near the New Mexico-Colorado border, huge piles of lava were erupted 8 to 2 million years ago onto an older, higher surface on top of either the Ogallala Formation of Miocene age or the Poison Canyon Formation of Paleocene age. (See table 1.) These lava flows formed a resistant cap, which protected the underlying rock from erosion while all the surrounding rock washed away. The result is the high, flat-topped mesas, such as Raton Mesa and Mesa de Maya (fig. 13), that now form the divide between the Arkansas and Canadian Rivers. At Fishers Peak, on the west end of Raton Mesa, about 800 feet of basalt flows rest on the Poison Canyon Formation at about 8,800 feet in altitude. Farther east, on Mesa de Maya, about 400 feet of basalt flows overlie the Ogallala Formation at altitudes ranging from about 6,500 feet at the west end to about 5,200 feet at the east end, some 35 miles to the east. The Ogallala here rests on Cretaceous Dakota Sandstone and Purgatoire Formation, for the Poison Canyon Formation was removed by erosion along the crest of a local uplift before the Ogallala was deposited.

East of the belt of upturned sedimentary layers that form the hogback ridges at the front of the Rocky Mountains, the layered rocks in the Raton Basin have been intruded in many

Figure 12. – Capulin Volcano National Monument in northeastern New Mexico. This huge cinder cone, which erupted between 4,000 and 10,000 years ago, rises more than 1,000 feet above its base. Photograph by R. D. Miller, U.S. Geological Survey.

Figure 13. – Lava-capped Mesa de Maya, east of Trinidad, Colo, Spanish Peaks in left distance. Mesa rises about 1,000 feet above surrounding area. Photograph by R. B. Taylor, U.S. Geological Survey.

places by igneous bodies, the two largest of which form the Spanish Peaks (fig. 14), southwest of Walsenburg, Colo. These two peaks are formed by igneous bodies that were intruded 26 to 22 million years ago and have since been exposed by removal of the overlying sedimentary rock layers by erosion. Radiating from the Spanish Peaks are hundreds of dikes, nearly vertical slabs of igneous rock that filled fractures radiating from the centers of intrusion. Erosion of the sedimentary layers has left many of these dikes as conspicuous vertical walls of igneous rock that project high above the surrounding land surface. Some of these dikes north of Trinidad, Colo, extend eastward for about 25 miles, almost to the Purgatoire River.

The northern boundary of the Raton section is placed somewhat indefinitely at the northern limit of the area injected by igneous dikes. The eastern boundary of the Raton section is at the eastern margin of the lavas of Mesa de Maya and adjoining mesas, where lava-capped outliers of Ogallala Formation are separated from the Ogallala of the High Plains only by the canyon of Carrizo Creek.

High Plains

At the end of Ogallala deposition, some 5 million years ago, the Great Plains, with the exception of the uplifted and the volcanic areas, was a vast, gently sloping plain that extended from the mountain front eastward to beyond the present Missouri River in some places. Regional uplift of the western part of the continent forced the streams to cut downward;

25

Figure 14. – Spanish Peaks, southwest of Walsenburg, Colo. Igneous intrusive rocks and many radiating dikes exposed by erosion. Photograph by R. B. Taylor, U.S. Geological Survey.

land near the mountains were stripped away by the Missouri, the Platte, the Arkansas, and the Pecos Rivers, and the eastern border of the plains was gnawed away by lesser streams. A large central area of the plain is preserved, however, essentially untouched and unaffected by the streams, as a little-modified remnant of the depositional surface of 5 million years ago. This Ogallala-capped preserved remnant of that upraised surface is the High Plains. In only one place does that old surface still extend to the mountains – at the so-called "Gangplank" west of Cheyenne, Wyo. (fig. 15)

Figure 15. – Looking eastward toward Cheyenne at "the Gangplank." Interstate Highway 80 and the Union Pacific Railroad follow the Gangplank from the High Plains in the distance onto the Precambrian rocks (older than 570 m.y.) of the Laramie Mountains in the foreground. Photograph by R. D. Miller, U.S. Geological Survey.

Figure 16. – Aerial view of the Scotts Bluff National Monument, Nebr. Buttes on the south side of the valley of the North Platte River isolated by erosion from High Plains in the background. Highest butte stands about 800 feet above valley floor.

In places, as at Scotts Bluff National Monument, Nebr. (fig 16), small fragments of this surface have been isolated from the High Plains by erosion and now stand above the surrounding area as buttes.

The High Plains extends southward from the Pine Ridge escarpment, near the South Dakota-Nebraska border (fig. 3), to the Edwards Plateau in Texas. The Platte, the Arkansas, and the Canadian Rivers have cut through the High Plains. That part of the High Plains south of the Canadian River is called the Southern High Plains, or the Llano Estacado (staked plain). The origin of this name is uncertain, but it has been suggested that the term Llano Estacado was applied by early travelers because this part of the High Plains is so nearly flat and devoid of landmarks that it was necessary for those pioneers to set lines of stakes to permit them to retrace their routes.

The Llano Estacado is bounded on the west by the Mescalero escarpment (fig. 4) and on the east by the Caprock escarpment. The southern margin with the Edwards Plateau is less well defined, but King Mountain, north of McCamey, Tex., is a scarp-bounded southern promontory of the High Plains. The remarkably flat surface of the Llano Estacado is abundantly pitted by sinks and depressions in the surface of the Ogallala Formation; these were formed by solution of the limestone by rainwater and blowing away or deflation by wind of the remaining insoluble particles. Many of these solution-deflation depressions are aligned like strings of beads, suggesting that their location is controlled by some kind of underlying structure, such as intersections of joints in the Ogallala Formation.

The solution-deflation depressions are less abundant north of the Canadian River, but occur on the High Plains surface northward to the Arkansas River and along the eastern part of the High Plains north of the Arkansas to the South Fork of the Republican River.

Covering much of the northern High Plains, however, are sand dunes and windblown silt deposits (loess) that mantle the Ogallala Formation and conceal any solution-deflation depressions that might have formed. The Nebraska Sand Hills (fig. 17), the largest area of sand dunes in the western hemisphere, is a huge area of stabilized sand dunes that extends from the White River in South Dakota southward

Figure 17. – Aerial view, looking northwest, of the Nebraska Sand Hills west of Ashby, Nebr.

beyond the Platte River almost to the Republican River in western Nebraska but only to the Loup River in the northeast part of the High Plains (fig. 18). Loess covers the western High Plains southward from the sand dunes almost to the Arkansas River, and to the South Fork of the Republican in the eastern part. This extensive cover of loess has created a fertile land that makes it an important part of America's wheatlands (fig. 19).

Other, smaller areas of sand dunes lie south of the Arkansas River valley. The only large areas of sand dunes on the Llano Estacado, or Southern High Plains, are along the southwestern margin near Monahans, southwest of Odessa, Tex.

Oil and gas are present in the Paleozoic rocks that underlie the High Plains at depth. Gas fields are ubiquitous in much of the eastern part of the High Plains between the Arkansas and Canadian Rivers. Just south of the Canadian River, at the northeast corner of the Southern High Plains, a huge oil and gas field has been developed near Pampa, Tex. Oil and gas fields also are abundant in the southwestern part of the Southern High Plains, south of Littlefield, Tex.

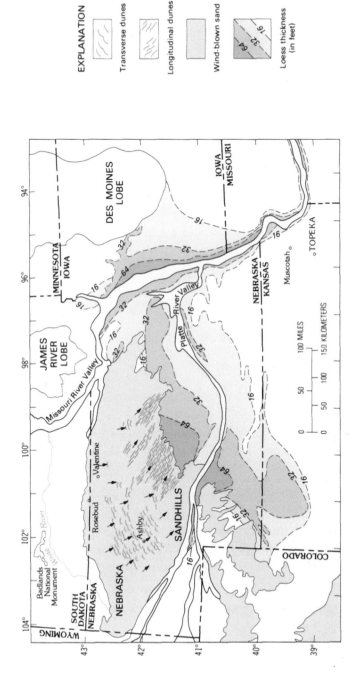

Figure 18. – The Sand Hills Region of Nebraska. Arrows show inferred direction of dune-forming winds. Map from Wright (1970), used by permission.

31

Figure 19. – Little-modified loess plain in southeastern Nebraska. Photograph by Judy Miller.

The surface of the High Plains, then, has been little modified by streams since the end of the Ogallala deposition. It has been raised by regional uplift and pitted by solution and deflation, and large parts of it have been covered by wind-blown sand and silt. It has been drilled for oil and gas and extensively farmed, but it is still a geological rarity – a preserved land surface that is 5 million years old.

Missouri Plateau

Beginning about 5 million years ago, regional uplift of the western part of the continent forced streams, which for 30 million years had been depositing sediment nearly continuously on the Great Plains, to change their behavior and begin to cut into the layers of sediment they so long had been depositing. The predecessor of the Missouri River ate headward into the northern Great Plains and developed a tributary system that excavated deeply into the accumulated deposits near the mountain front and carried away huge volumes of sediment from the Great Plains to Hudson Bay. By 2 million years ago, the streams had cut downward to within a few hundred feet of their present level. This region that has been so thoroughly dissected by the Missouri River and its tributaries is called the Missouri Plateau.

About 2 million years ago, after much downcutting had already taken place and river channels had been firmly established, great ice sheets advanced southward from Canada into the United States. (See figure 2.) These continental glaciers formed, advanced, and retreated several times during the last 2 million years. At the north and east margins of the Missouri Plateau they lapped onto a high area, leaving a mantle of glacial deposits covering the bedrock surface and forcing streams to adopt new courses along the margin of ice. The part of the Missouri Plateau covered by the continental glaciers now is referred to as the Glaciated Missouri Plateau. South of the part once covered by ice is the Unglaciated Missouri Plateau.

Preglacial Drainage

Before the initial advance of the continental ice sheets, the Missouri River flowed northeastward into Canada and to Hudson Bay. Its major tributaries, the Yellowstone and the Little Missouri joined the Missouri in northwestern North Dakota. The east-flowing Knife, Heart, and Cannonball Rivers in North Dakota also joined a stream that flowed northward to Hudson Bay.

Glaciated Missouri Plateau

When the continental ice sheets spread southward into northern Montana and the Dakotas, a few isolated areas in Montana stood above the surrounding plain. These are mostly areas that were uplifted by the intrusion of igneous bodies long before the streams began downcutting and carving the land. The northernmost of these isolated mountains, the Sweetgrass Hills, were surrounded by ice and became nunataks, or islands of land, in the sea of advancing ice, which pushed southward up against the Highwood Mountains, near Great Falls, the Bearpaws south of Havre, and the Little Rockies to the east.

Much of the northern part of Montana is a plain of little relief that is the surface of a nearly continuous cover of glacial deposits, generally less than 50 feet thick. This plain has been incised by the east-flowing postglacial Teton, Marias, and Milk Rivers.

In North Dakota, a high area on the east side of the Williston basin acted as a barrier to the advance of the ice, most of which was diverted southeastward. The margin of the ice sheet, however, lapped onto the bedrock high, where it stagnated. Earlier advances moved farthest south; the later advances stopped north of the present course of the Missouri River – their maximum position marked by ridges of unsorted, glacially transported rock debris (till) called terminal moraines. North of the terminal moraines is a distinctive landscape characterized by a rolling, hummocky, or hilly surface with thousands of closed depressions between the hills and hummocks, most of them occupied by lakes. This is the deposit left by the stagnant or dead ice, and it is called dead-ice moraine. The rolling upland in North Dakota that is covered by dead-ice moraine and ridges of terminal moraine from the last glacial advances is called the Coteau du Missouri (fig. 20). A gently sloping scarp, several hundred feet high and mostly covered by glacial deposits (referred to collectively as drift), separates the Coteau du Missouri from the lower, nearly flat, drift-covered plains of the Central Lowland to the east. This escarpment, which is called the Missouri escarpment, is virtually continuous across the State of North Dakota southward into South Dakota. The base of the Missouri escarpment is the eastern boundary of the Great Plains in these northern states.

Figure 20. – Ground moraine on the Coteau du Missouri, northwestern North Dakota. Photograph by R.M. Lindvall, U.S. Geological Survey.

The advancing ice front blocked one after another of the northward-flowing streams of the region, diverting them eastward along the ice front. Shonkin Sag, north of the Highwood Mountains near Great Falls, Mont., is an abandoned diversion channel of the Missouri River, occupied when the ice front stood close to the north slopes of the Highwoods. Much of the present course of the Missouri River from Great Falls, Mont., to Kansas City, Mo., was established as an ice-marginal channel, and the east-flowing part of the Little Missouri River in North Dakota was formed in the same way. These valleys were cut during the last 2 million years.

The north-flowing part of the Little Missouri River and the east-flowing courses of the Knife, Heart, and Cannonball Rivers in North Dakota are for the most part older, preglacial courses. The Little Missouri was dammed by the ice, and its waters impounded to form a huge lake during the maximum stand of the ice, but the deposits of this glacial lake are few and make no imprint on the landscape.

The valley of the east-flowing, glacially diverted part of the Little Missouri River, however, is markedly different from that of the north-flowing preglacial river. It is much narrower and has steeper walls than the old valley. Because it is younger, it is little modified, except by huge landslides that have affected both walls of the valley. Tremendous rotated landslide blocks in the North Unit of Theodore Roosevelt National Park are some of the best examples of the slump type of landslide to be seen anywhere (fig. 21).

Melting ice at the front of the glaciers provided large volumes of meltwater that flowed across the till-mantled surface in front of the glacier as it melted back toward Canada. This meltwater took many courses to join the glacially diverted Missouri River, and these sinuous meltwater channels wind across the dead-ice moraine and the older, less hummocky ground moraine between the Coteau du Missouri and the Missouri River. Locally the sediment carried by the meltwater streams was banked against a wall of ice to form a small hill of stratified drift that is called a kame. Streams flowing in tunnels beneath the ice formed sinuous, ridgelike deposits called eskers, and in places the meltwater deposits form broad flat areas called outwash plains.

Figure 21. – Rotated slump blocks in huge landslide, North Unit of Theodore Roosevelt National Park, N.Dak. Note that layering of Fort Union Formation in cliffs on skyline, where landslide originated, is horizontal.

This rather limited variety of landforms, then, characterizes the landscape of the Glaciated Missouri Plateau. The landforms themselves are testimony to their glacial origin and to the great advances of the continental ice sheets. This is a stream-carved terrain that has been modified by continental glaciers and almost completely covered by a thick blanket of glacially transported and deposited rock debris, locally hundreds of feet thick. Subsequent stream action has not altered the landscape greatly.

Unglaciated Missouri Plateau

Beyond the limits reached by the ice of the continental glaciers, the Unglaciated Missouri Plateau displays the greatest variety of landforms of any section of the Great Plains. In western Montana, many small mountain masses rise above the general level of the plateau, including the Highwood, Bearpaw, and Little Rocky Mountains near the

Figure 22. – The Highwood Mountains seen from the Little Belt Mountains, Mont. Photography by I. J. Witkind, U.S. Geological Survey.

margin of the glaciated area, and the Judith, Big Snowy, Big Belt, Little Belt, Castle, and Crazy Mountains farther south (fig. 22). Many of these, such as the Crazy, Castle, Judith, and Big Snowy Mountains, are areas uplifted by large, deeply rooted, intrusive igneous bodies called stocks, which have been exposed by subsequent erosion of the arched overlying sedimentary rock layers. Some, such as the Highwood and Bearpaw Mountains, are predominantly piles of lava flows, although in the Bearpaws the related intrusive bodies of igneous rock form a part of the mountains. The Big and Little Belt Mountains were formed by mushroom-shaped intrusive igneous bodies call laccoliths, which have spread out and domed between layers of sedimentary rocks. A number of igneous bodies also intrude the rocks of the Missouri Plateau around the periphery of the Black Hills. Devils Tower, the first feature to be designated a National Monument, is the best known of these igneous rock features (fig. 23).

The uplift and volcanism that formed these mountains took place before the streams began to cut downward and segment the Great Plains. The mountains had been greatly dissected before the advent of the Great Ice Age, when alpine glaciers formed on the Castle and the Crazy Mountains and flowed down some of the stream-cut valleys. Alpine glacial features such as cirques, in the high parts of the mountains, and glacially modified U-shaped valleys (fig. 24) are impressive evidence of this glaciation.

Figure 23. – Devils Tower National Monument, Wyo. An igneous intrusive body exposed by erosion. Photograph by F. W. Osterwald, U.S. Geological Survey.

Figure 24. – U-shaped, glaciated valley of Big Timber Creek, Crazy Mountains, Mont. Photo courtesy of U.S. Forest Service.

The Missouri River and its tributaries – the Sun, Smith, Judith, Musselshell, and Yellowstone Rivers in Montana and the Little Missouri River in North Dakota – have cut down into the Missouri Plateau, cut broad upland surfaces at many levels, and established confined valleys with valley floors flanked by terrace remnants of older floodplains. Locally, high buttes that are remnants of former interstream divides rise above the uplands. Large lakes also were formed in most of these tributary valleys because of damming by the continental ice sheets.

West of the Black Hills, in Wyoming, the Tongue River and the Powder River have excavated the Powder River Basin and produced similar features (fig. 25). The east-flowing tributaries of the Missouri River – the Knife, Heart, and Cannonball Rivers in North Dakota and the Grand, Moreau, Belle Fourche, Cheyenne, Bad, and White Rivers in South Dakota – similarly have shaped the landscape.

Most of these rivers flow in broad, old valleys, established more than 2 million years ago, before the first advance of the continental ice sheets. Some of these valleys have been widened by recession of the valley walls by badland development. Badlands are formed by the cutting action of rivulets and rills flowing down over a steeply sloping face of soft, fine-grained material composed mainly of clay and

Figure 25. – View northeast across the Deckers coal mine and the Tongue River in the Powder River Basin, southeastern Montana. Typical terrain of unglaciated Missouri Plateau. Small mesas with cliffed escarpments on capping layer of resistant sandstone, such as those in the foreground, are common. Coal mine is about 1 mile across. Photograph by R. B. Taylor, U.S. Geological Survey.

silt. The intricate carving by thousands of small streams of water produces the distinctive rounded and gullied terrain we call badlands. Badlands National Park in South Dakota (fig. 26) has been established in the remarkable badlands terrain cut into the White River Group along the north valley wall of the White River, and the South Unit of Theodore Roosevelt National Park is in the colorful badlands of the Little Missouri River, formed on the Fort Union Formation (fig. 27).

The White River also has cut a steep scarp along its southern wall that is called the Pine Ridge escarpment. This escarpment defines the boundary between the Missouri Plateau and the High Plains here.

The landscape of the Unglaciated Missouri Plateau has been determined largely by the action of streams, but in some

Figure 26. – Badlands in Badlands National Park, S. Dak. Photograph by W. H. Raymond, III. U.S. Geological Survey.

40

Figure 27. – Badlands of the Little Missouri River in South Unit of Theodore Roosevelt National Park, N. Dak. View looking northwest from near Painted Canyon Overlook along Interstate 94, west of Belfield. Photo courtesy of Bruce Kaye.

areas igneous intrusions and volcanoes have produced small mountain masses that interrupt the plain, and valley glaciers have modified the valleys in some of these mountains.

The Colorado Piedmont

The Colorado Piedmont lies in the eastern foot of the Rockies, (fig. 1) largely between the South Platte River and the Arkansas River. The South Platte on the north and the Arkansas River on the south, after leaving the mountains, have excavated deeply into the Tertiary (65- to 2-million-year-old) sedimentary rock layers of the Great Plains in Colorado and removed great volumes of sediment. At Denver, the South Platte River has cut downward 1,500 to 2,000 feet to its present level. Three well-formed terrace levels flank the river's floodplain, and remnants of a number of well-formed higher land surfaces are preserved between the river and the mountains. Along the western margin of the Colorado Piedmont, the layers of older sedimentary rock have been sharply upturned by the rise of the mountains. The eroded edges of these upturned layers have been eroded differentially, so that the hard sandstone and limestone layers form conspicuous and continuous hogback ridges (fig. 28). North of the South Platte River, near the Wyoming border, a scarp that has been cut on the rocks of the High

Plains marks the northern boundary of the Colorado Piedmont. Pawnee Buttes (fig. 29) are two of many butte outliers of the High Plains rocks near that scarp, separated from the High Plains by erosion as is Scotts Bluff, farther north in Nebraska. To the east, about 10 miles northwest of Limon, Colo., Cedar Point forms a west-jutting prow of the High Plains.

The Arkansas River similarly has excavated much of the Tertiary piedmont deposits and cut deeply into the older Cretaceous marine rocks between Canon City and the Kansas border. The upturned layers along the mountain front, marked by hogback ridges and intervening valleys, continue nearly uninterrupted around the south end of the Front Range into the embayment in the mountains at Canon City. Skyline Drive, a scenic drive at Canon City, follows the crest of the Dakota hogback for a short distance and provides a fine panorama of the Canon City embayment.

Extending eastward from the mountain front at Palmer Lake, a high divide separates the drainage of the South Platte River from that of the Arkansas River. The crest of the divide

Figure 28. – Hogback ridges along the Front Range west of Denver, Colo. South Platte River emerges from the mountains and cuts through hogbacks in middle distance. Photograph courtesy of Eugene Shearer, Intrasearch, Inc.

north of Colorado Springs is generally between 7,400 and 7,600 feet in altitude, but Interstate Highway 25 crosses it about 7,350 feet, nearly 1,500 feet higher than Colorado Springs and more than 2,000 feet higher than Denver. From the crest of the divide to north of Castle Rock, resistant Oligocene Castle Rock Conglomerate (which is equivalent to part of the White River Group of the High Plains) is preserved in many places and forms a protective caprock on mesas and buttes. This picturesque part of the Colorado Piedmont looks quite different from the excavated valleys of the South Platte and Arkansas Rivers.

Much of the terrain in the two river valleys has been smoothed by a nearly continuous mantle of windblown sand and silt. Northwesterly winds, which frequently blow with near-hurricane velocities, have whipped fine material from the floodplains of the streams and spread it eastward and

Figure 29. – Pawnee Buttes in northeastern Colorado. Buttes isolated by erosion from High Plains in the background. Ogallala Formation caps top of Buttes. White River Group forms lower part. The top of the highest butte is about 240 feet above the saddle between the two buttes. Photograph by R. D. Miller, U.S. Geological Survey.

southeastward over much of the Colorado Piedmont. Well-formed dunes are not common, but alined gentle ridges of sand and silt and abundant shallow blowout depressions inform us of the windblown origin of this cover. In the Colorado Piedmont, then, the erosional effects of streams are the most conspicuous features of the landscape, but these are enhanced by the steep tilting of the layered rocks along the western margin as a result of earth movement and modified by the nearly ubiquitous products of wind action, which have softened the landscape with a widespread cover of windblown sand and silt.

Pecos Valley

South of the land of volcanic rocks that is the Raton section, the Pecos River has cut a broad valley from the Sangre de Cristo Mountains, in New Mexico, southward to the Rio Grande, and has removed the piedmont cover of Ogallala Formation and cut deeply into the underlying rocks. The Ogallala Formation capping the High Plains to the east forms a rimrock at the top of the sharp Mescalero escarpment, which is the eastern boundary of the Pecos Valley. (See figure 4.) The western boundary of the Pecos Valley is the eastern base of discontinuous mountain ranges.

The great thickness of Tertiary deposits that formed on the northern Great Plains did not accumulate here, and the Pecos River has cut its valley into the older marine sedimentary rocks. The rocks underlying the surface of much of the Pecos Valley are upper Paleozoic limestones.

The soluble nature of limestone is responsible for some of the most spectacular features of the landscape in the Pecos Valley. For about 10 miles north and 50 miles south of Vaughn, N. Mex., collapsed solution caverns in upper Paleozoic limestones have produced an unusual type of topography called karst. Karst topography is typified by numerous closely spaced sinks or closed depressions, some of which are very deep holes, caused by the collapse of the roof of a cave or solution cavity into the underground void, leaving hills, spines, or hummocks at the top of the intervening walls or ribs separating the depressions.

Although the karst in the vicinity of Vaughn is perhaps the most conspicuous solution phenomenon, sinks and caves are common throughout the Pecos Valley. At Bottomless Lakes State Park east of Roswell, N. Mex., seven lakes occupy large sinkholes caused by the solution of salt and gypsum in underlying rocks.

The most spectacular example of solution of limestone by ground water is Carlsbad Caverns, N. Mex., one of the most beautiful caves in the world. This celebrated solution cavity is preserved in a national park.

The Pecos River along much of its present course flows in a vertical-walled canyon with limestone rims. The Canadian River, flowing eastward from the Sangre de Cristo Mountains, has cut a deep canyon along the northern part of the Pecos Valley section. The sharp rims of the Dakota Sandstone at the Canadian escarpment, north of the Canadian River, form the northern boundary of the Pecos Valley section.

The sharp, northeast-trending broken flexure called the Border Hills that is crossed by U.S. Highway 70-380 about 20 miles west of Roswell is a unique landform of the Pecos Valley. This markedly linear upfolded (anticlinal) structure forms a ridge more than 30 miles long and about 200 feet high.

As in the Colorado Plateau, windblown sand and silt mantle the landscape in many places, but the greatest accumulations are along the base of the Mescalero escarpment at the northeast and southeast corners of the Pecos Valley section.

East of the Pecos River, in the southeast part of the Pecos Valley, the underlying rocks have yielded much oil and potash. Oil fields are common east of Artesia and Carlsbad, and potash is mined east of Carlsbad.

The Pecos and Canadian Rivers and their tributaries have created the general outline of the landscape of the Pecos Valley, but underground solution of limestone by ground water and the collapse of roofs of these cavities have contributed much detail to the surface that characterizes the Pecos Valley today.

Edwards Plateau

South of the Pecos Valley section, the Pecos River continues its journey to the Rio Grande in a steep-walled

Figure 30. – Rio Grande and the flat-lying limestone layers of the Edwards Plateau downstream from the mouth of the Pecos River. Mexico on the left side of picture. Photograph courtesy of National Park Service, Amistad Recreation Area.

canyon cut 400 to 500 feet below the level of a plateau surface of Cretaceous limestone from which little has been stripped except a thin Tertiary cover of Ogallala Formation (fig. 30). To the east, the plateau has been similarly incised by the Devils River and the West Nueces and Nueces Rivers. East of the Nueces to the escarpment formed by the Balcones fault zone, the southern part of the Edwards Plateau has been intricately dissected by the Frio, Sabinal, Medina, Guadalupe, and Pedernales Rivers and their tributary systems. San Antonio and Austin, Tex., are located on the Coastal Plain at the edge of the Balcones fault zone.

The Pecos River, and to a lesser extent the Devils and Nueces Rivers, particularly in their lower courses, have entrenched themselves deeply in the plateau in remarkable meandering courses of a type that is usually found only in broad, low-lying floodplains. These stream courses reflect the stream environment prior to regional uplift.

Sinkholes pit the relatively undissected limestone plateau surface in the northeast part of the Edwards Plateau, and some underground solution cavities in the limestone are well-known caves, such as the Caverns of Sonora, southwest of Sonora, Tex.

Oil and gas fields are widely developed in the northern part of the Edwards Plateau, but only cattle ranches are found in the bare southern part.

Ancient oceans deposited the limestones that now cap the Edwards Plateau; streams planed off the surface of the flat-lying limestone layers and entrenched themselves in steep-walled valleys; and ground water dissolved the limestone and created the solution cavities that are the caves and sinks of the Edwards Plateau. Water has created this landscape.

Plains Border Section

The Missouri Plateau, the Colorado Piedmont, the Pecos Valley, and the Edwards Plateau all were outlined by streams that flowed from the mountains. On the eastern border of the Great Plains, however, headward cutting by streams that have their source areas in the High Plains has dissected a large area, mainly in Kansas. This Plains Border Section comprises a number of east-trending river valleys – of the Republican, Solomon, Saline, Smoky Hill, Arkansas, Medicine Lodge, Cimarron, and North Canadian Rivers – and interstream divides, most of which are intricately dissected.

North of the Arkansas River, the east-flowing Republican, Solomon, Saline, and Smoky Hill Rivers have incised themselves a few hundred feet below the Tertiary High Plains surface and have developed systems of closely spaced tributary draws. The interstream divides are narrow, and the tributary heads nearly meet at the divides. This intricately dissected part of the Plains Border section is called the Smoky Hills. Some isolated buttes of Cretaceous rocks left in the upper valley of the Smoky Hill River are called the Monument Rocks. A large area of rounded boulders exposed by erosion south of the Solomon River, southwest of Minneapolis, Kans., is called "Rock City." These boulders originated as resistant nodules (concretions) within the Cretaceous rocks that contained them.

South of the Arkansas River is a broad, nearly flat upland sometimes referred to as the Great Bend Plains. The Medicine Lodge River has cut headward into the southeastern part of the Great Bend Plains and created a thoroughly dissected topography in Triassic red rocks that is locally called the Red Hills. In a few places, badlands have formed in the Red Hills.

Some large sinks or collapse depressions have formed because of solution of salt and gypsum at depth by ground water. Big and Little Basins, in Clark County in southcentral Kansas, were formed in this way.

Sand dunes have accumulated in places, especially near stream valleys. Dunes are common, for example, along the north side of the North Canadian River.

Oil and gas fields are widely developed in the southeast part of the Plains Border section – in the Smoky Hills, the Great Bend Plains and the Red Hills.

The Plains Border section, like the Missouri Plateau, the Colorado Piedmont, and the Pecos Valley, is primarily a product of stream dissection. The differences in the outstanding landforms of the section are mainly the result of differences in the hardness of the eroded rocks.

Epilogue

The Great Plains, as we have seen, is many things. It contains thick layers of rock that formed in oceans, and younger layers of rocks deposited by streams. These rocks have been affected by earth movements and injected by hot molten rock, some of which reached the surface as volcanic rock. The rocks have been carved by streams, dissolved by ground water, partly covered by glaciers, and blown by winds. All of these agents have played important roles in determining the landscape and the land forms of the Great Plains. But the streams were the master agent. They formed the great depositional plain that was to become the Great Plains, and then began to destroy it – leaving only the High Plains to remind us of what it was. Those long miles we travel across the High Plains are a journey through history – geologic history.

Acknowledgments

This narrative history of geologic and biologic events in the Great Plains had its origin in a study intended to identify

49

potential National Natural Landmarks in the Great Plains, commissioned by the National Park Service. William A. Cobban, G. Edward Lewis, and Reuben J. Ross of the U.S. Geological Survey were collaborators in that study, and some of their contributions to the history of life on the Great Plains have been incorporated into this narrative, which was undertaken at the urging of Wallace R. Hansen. The photographic illustrations, other than those obtained from the film library of the U.S. Geological Survey, were provided by the interest and effort of my friends and colleagues of the Geological Survey – including C.R. Dunrud, V.L. Freeman, C.D. Miller, R.D. Miller, F.W. Osterwald, R.L. Parker, W.H. Raymond, III, Kenneth Shaver, and R.B. Taylor – and by Eugene Shearer, Intrasearch, Inc., Denver, Colo. Without their help this publication would not have been possible.

Some Source References

Alden, W.C., 1932, Physiography and glacial geology of eastern Montana and adjacent areas: U.S. Geological Survey Professional Paper 174, 133 p.
Bluemle, J.P., 1988, North Dakota Geological Highway Map: North Dakota Geological Survey.
Bluemle, J.P., 1977, The face of North Dakota – the geologic story: North Dakota Geological Survey Education Series 11, 73 p.
Colton, R.B., Lemke, R.W., and Lindvall, R.M., 1961, Glacial map of Montana east of the Rocky Mountains: U.S. Geological Survey Miscellaneous Geologic Investigations Map I-327.
Colton, R.B., Lemke, R.W., and Lindvall, R.M., 1963, Preliminary glacial map of North Dakota: U.S. Geological Survey Miscellaneous Geologic Investigations Map I-331.
Curtis, B.F., ed., 1975, Cenozoic history of the southern Rocky Mountains – Papers deriving from a symposium presented at Rocky Mountain Section meeting of the Geological Society of America, Boulder, Colorado, 1973: Geological Survey of America Memoir 144, 279 p.
Darton, N.H., 1905, Preliminary report on the geology and underground water resources of the central Great Plains: U.S. Geological Survey Professional Paper 32, 433 p.
Flint, R.F., 1955, Pleistocene geology of eastern South Dakota: U.S. Geological Survey Professional Paper 262, 173 p.

Frye, J.C., and Leonard, A.B., 1965, Quaternary of the southern Great Plains, *in* Wright, H.E., Jr., and Frey, D.G., eds., The Quaternary of the United States – A review volume for the 7th Congress of the International Association of Quaternary Research: Princeton University Press, p. 203-216.

Howard, A.D., 1958, Drainage evolution in northeastern Montana and northwestern North Dakota: Geological Society of America Bulletin, v. 69, no. 5, p. 575-588.

Johnson, R.B., 1961, Patterns and origin of radial dike swarms associated with West Spanish Peak and Dike Mountain, south-central Colorado: Geological Society of America Bulletin, v. 72, no. 4, p. 579-590.

Judson, S.S., Jr., 1950, Depressions of the northern portion of the southern High Plains of eastern New Mexico: Geological Society of America Bulletin, v. 61, no. 3, p. 253-274.

Keech, C.F., and Bentall, Ray, 1971, Dunes on the plains – The Sand Hills region of Nebraska: Nebraska University Conservation and Survey Division Resources Report 4, 18 p.

Lemke, R.W., Laird, W.M., Tipton, M.J., and Lindvall, R.M., 1965, Quaternary geology of northern Great Plains, *in* Wright, H.E., Jr., and Frey, D.G., eds., The Quaternary of the United States – A review volume for the 7th Congress of the International Association for Quaternary Research: Princeton University Press, p. 15-27.

Mansfield, G.R., 1907, Glaciation in the Crazy Mountains of Montana: Geological Society of America Bulletin, v. 19, p. 558-567.

Oetking, P.; Renfro, H.B.; Feray, D.E.; and Bennison, A.P.; Geological Highway Maps for the Regions: Great Plains; Mid-Continent; and Texas.

Pettyjohn, W.A., 1966, Eocene paleosol in the northern Great Plains, *in* Geological Survey Research 1966: U.S. Geological Survey Professional Paper 550-C, p. C61-C65.

Robinson, C.S., 1956, Geology of Devils Tower National Monument, Wyoming: U.S. Geological Survey Bulletin 1021-I, p. 289-302.

Stormer, J.C., Jr., 1972, Ages and nature of volcanic activity on the southern High Plains, New Mexico and Colorado: Geological Society of America Bulletin, v. 83, no. 8, p. 2443-2448.

Strahler, A.N., and Strahler, A.H., 1978, Modern physical geography: New York, John Wiley & Sons, 502 p.

Thornbury, W.D., 1965, Regional geomorphology of the United States: New York, John Wiley, 609 p.

Wright, H.E., Jr., 1970, Vegetational history of the Central Plains, *in* Pleistocene and recent environments of the central Great Plains: Kansas University Department of Geology Special Publication 3, p. 157-172.

Index

(Italic page numbers indicate major references)